thecollective
Contemporary Styles Series

T0085534

The Roots of Groove:
R&B/Soul & Contemporary Funk Styles For the Drums

by Pat Petrillo

thecollective is a world-class learning center for drumset players, percussionists, bassists, keyboardists and guitarists of all levels. We offer plans of study ranging from individual lessons and clinics to full-time programs of ten weeks to two years in length. If you're serious about becoming the best musician you can be, we're serious about helping you accomplish that goal.

**541 Avenue of the Americas,
New York, NY 10011
T: 212-741-0091**   **www.thecoll.com**

Executive Producer – *Lauren Keiser*
Executive Co-producer – *John Castellano*
Author Liason – *Tony Maggiolino*
Creative Director – *Alex Teploff*
Managing Editor – *Nicholas Hopkins*
Production Editor – *Joe Bergamini*
Cover Design – *Andrew J. Dowty*
Book Design – *Andrew J. Dowty*
Production Designer – *Andy Ray Wong*
Photo of New York City – *Maureen Plainfield*
Other Photography – *Andy Dowty and Kyung Chul-Choi*
Production Coordinator and Audio Engineer – *Tony Conniff*

CARL FISCHER®
65 Bleecker Street, New York, NY 10012

ISBN 0-8258-6271-X

TABLE OF CONTENTS

Performers on the CD:

Bass: Frank Gravis

Guitar on Tracks 1-8, 20: Chris Biesterfeld

Guitar on Tracks 9-19, 21, 22: Jerome Covington

Keyboards on Tracks 1-8, 20: Dan Rosengard

Keyboards on Tracks 9-19, 21, 22: Sharp Radway

FOREWORD

The Collective was established in 1977 by a small group of professional New York musicians, who wanted to pool their energies and create a place where young drummers, and later bass, guitar, and keyboard students, could study and prepare themselves for a career in music. Since opening its doors, The Collective has graduated thousands of students, who have gone on to establish themselves in the world of professional music. I don't think that it is immodest to say that our alumni are helping to shape the direction that popular music is taking around the world.

Over the years the curriculum at The Collective has evolved to include a wide range of courses focusing on everything from technique and reading, to the study of all the important contemporary and ethnic styles. This book, along with our other Rhythm Section based books, covers the material offered in the Collective's Certificate Program.

The styles offered here represent the key styles in the contemporary idiom. Since all styles have tended to grow out of each other, and mutually influence each other, the student will find common threads that link them all together and make it easier to absorb and make them part of a young musician's personal style signature.

Each book contains a brief biography of the author, who is the faculty member who teaches this style at The Collective. You will also find a brief introduction to the general style and examples of the various substyles to be studied. Woven throughout the material are performance tips that come out of the teacher's years of experience. The most important element, however, are the pre-recorded rhythm-section CDs, on which our teachers perform with other musicians who also specialize in playing the style. Listening to and practicing with these CDs are the most important things for you to do to develop skills playing in the style. Music notation and the written word can, at best, only help you derive an intellectual understanding of the music. It is in listening to the actual music that you will come to understand it. In this regard, we strongly encourage you to make an effort to listen to the music listed in the recommended discography at the end of each section. The blank staves are meant for you to notate your own personal variations for each style. First, you must learn the pure style; then, you can adapt it to your own musical needs.

I would like to express my appreciation to all the teachers who have, over the years, contributed to the growth of the Collective and to this program in particular. I would also like to thank the hard working and talented folks at Carl Fischer for supporting our effort to get it right, and doing such a fine job with this book. Finally, I would like to thank Tony Maggiolino of our staff for all his hard work in coordinating all the material, and struggling to meet ever looming deadlines.

—John Castellano.
Director, The Collective

AUTHOR'S INTRODUCTION

This book covers a wide range of groove styles and sub-genres, from the roots of early R&B through Motown and into Contemporary Funk derivatives. These grooves are essential to becoming a successful, working drummer, and they will become the basis upon which you can develop many variations for years to come. In studying this music and its history, you will come to see how one sub-style influenced the next, and how there is a common thread that runs through them all. That thread is the *groove*.

Groove is hard to define, but the funny thing is, we know it when we hear it. It is this special feeling that is so elusive, yet speaks volumes, and makes this music unique. There will be many explanations in this book that may help better define terms like "pocket," the "lock," etc, but more than a mere explanation and definition are needed to truly understand this music. More than anything else, it must be experienced. So I encourage you to seek out the original recordings in the Discography that is provided on p. 28. Listen and play along to the original recordings. Transcribe the parts if you wish. But, I assure you, that will not be necessary.

You see, I began playing at age five by playing along to the music of The Beatles, and I got my first James Brown recording at age ten. I could not read music, nor transcribe it. I simply played along to the music and tried to let the feel and groove permeate my ears and soul. From those early days forward, up to this very day, I continually reach out and grab the next "branch" from the groove "tree," hold on for dear life, and just play along to the music. This music provides the inspiration and motivation, and that's what I hope to pass on to you.

Some teachers are of the opinion that you can't teach someone how to groove. I think you can help a drummer to find a groove, nurture it, shape and define it, and eventually it will be engrained into the subconscious and physical being. So, it is critical to continually listen to new groove music, with a tip of the cap to the past classics that have shaped today's sound, which will become tomorrow's classics. I hope you will always be as "funky as you *want* to be!"

—Pat Petrillo

ABOUT PAT PETRILLO

Pat is recognized as one of today's most prolific and versatile drummers, having performed and recorded with a wide variety of artists from many genres of music including R&B legends Gloria Gaynor and Patti LaBelle, to Pop/Rock artists Glen Burtnik and Patty Smyth, to Jazz artists Ed Hamilton and his group Groovallegiance featuring Chieli Minucci, Gary Grainger and Chris Fischer. He has also played numerous Broadway shows over the years, including *A Chorus Line, Grease, Footloose* and *Dreamgirls.*

Pat is also one of the most sought-after educators and clinicians in the business, and is a full-time faculty member at Drummers Collective in New York City. As a clinician and endorser for Zildjian cymbals, Remo drumheads and the S-Hoop drum hoop, he has conducted clinics and master classes all over the world. He is also an artist-in-residence at the University of North Carolina-Pembroke.

For more on Pat, visit **www.patpetrillo.com** or www.myspace.com/patpetrillo

Drumkey Notation

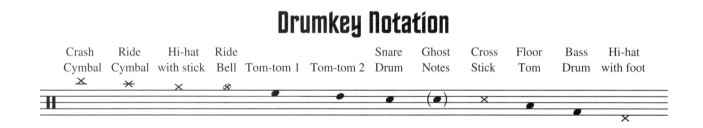

INTRODUCTION

Educational "PhilosoFunk" (How to Learn)

In education, *assimilation* is a very important method of developing musical awareness, perspective, and ultimately comprehension. It is sort of a "monkey see, monkey do" approach. In the same way, *memorization* is critical to learning specific concepts, whether they be theoretical or technical. Therefore, *internal comprehension* is a form of *deep memorization and assimilation* of concepts. There are three aspects to developing internal comprehension, which are the mental (theoretical), the physical (technical), and emotional (spiritual) disciplines. They are each independent *yet* interdependent of one another, for without any one of these three disciplines, a person cannot achieve an optimum performance level. However, of these three, the greatest value, in my opinion, is the emotional discipline, and this is the *root* of all great groove playing. This is why it all works. Listen to the originals, let them marinate, and begin your journey to becoming a better groove player.

The Methodology to the Madness

The groove examples I have created are inspired by all of the great musical grooves that have come before us. Each sub-style has a brief historical perspective, followed by detailed groove analysis and variations. The play-along tracks provide opportunity to perform with a live rhythm section. I strongly recommend that you memorize each groove so that the focus becomes *playing*, and not *reading*. As George Clinton once said, "Free your mind, and *the groove* will follow."…or something like that.

The sub-styles covered in this book are:

1) Early R&B Roots
2) The Grooves of Motown
3) Essential R&B/Soul
4) Essential Funk
6) Linear Funk
7) Go-Go, Hip Hop, New Jack Swing

How to Practice with This Book

By using a combination of three-minute songs and three-minute isolated groove examples, I feel that there is a mix of approaches to studying this style that will benefit your groove. Don't be misled by the relative technical "ease" of some of these grooves. Ultimately, the goal is *consistency* on a multitude of levels:

• of sound and projection
• of tempo and time
• of intensity
• of memory

These all have to be developed *at the same time*, and the only way to do that is with repetitive practice with these tracks. Just because you can read it and play, doesn't necessarily mean you can really *play* it! There is a big difference, so focus on the above elements at all times.

Groove Variations and Colorations

All of the grooves are written using the eighth note as a constant on the hi-hat, with the exception of the linear grooves in the last section. There are obviously other things you can add to the grooves during the chorus or bridge sections which raise the intensity and add color and shape to the music. Below are some "groove variations" which can be played on top of the bass and snare "shell groove." Try these over all of the grooves in the book and switch between the eighths on the hi-hat and any of these variations.

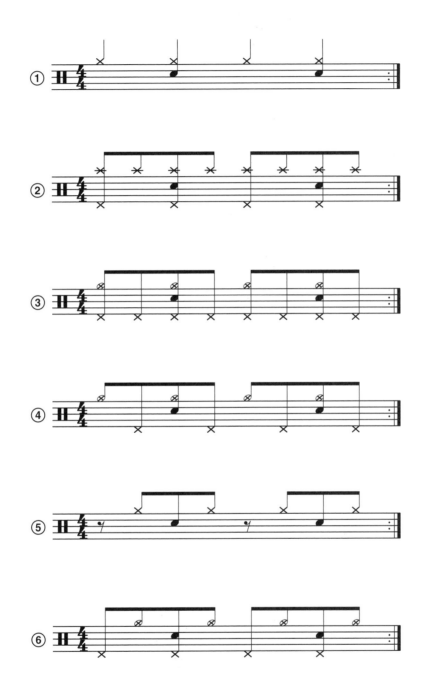

Defining the R&B Sound: Tuning and Concepts

The Snare-Drum Sound

This is critical to creating the right vibe for R&B and Funk. When I played with Patti LaBelle, as well as Gloria Gaynor, I used at least two snare drums, and sometimes three. A standard 5½" x 14" tuned open, then a 10" x 5" stainless-steel or brass "side snare" for a high pitched, tight crack, and yet another 13" x 6" for a fatter, dry, "old-school" sound, tuned lower, and that I always played right in the center. Each tune would require a specific sound, based on the type of snare used on the recording and the era in which it was recorded. The music always dictated my sound. Oftentimes, I would use all three in the same song for a "breakdown" section, or for various "ghosted" notes so that the sound differential was noticeable.

Rimshot or Not?

Yes…no…maybe…it depends. Again, the music decides, based on the dynamics, the vibe of the music, and what the engineer or producer wants for the song. If you are playing a live gig, a rimshot can totally cut through everything and become overbearing, especially in an unmiked situation. It is NOT a rule that you must play a rimshot when playing Funk or R&B. (Listen to Parliament/Funkadelic and see how many songs in which you hear a rimshot.) However, I would say that many times, in a Funk/Fusion setting, or Contemporary Gospel, the "crack" of the snare is the desired sound for the style. Just use your ears and instincts on this one.

The Bass-Drum Sound

Generally, the bass drum is deep, dry, thumpy, and has a nice attack, or "tic." I use a hard felt, round beater. This sound can be achieved by using a two-ply head with a muffling device inside or on the outside. I use the Remo Powersonic bass-drum head. Be sure that front head, or the head facing the audience, is also muffled slightly from the inside. To achieve the "tic" on the attack, I put a Remo falam slam on the head where the beater hits. Another factor that contributes to this sound is having a hole in the front head so that the air escapes. This is crucial to take out extra reverberation in the drum.

Some drummers prefer a "boomy" or "open" bass-drum sound, taking more of a Jazz approach. I believe this method of tuning is the exception rather than the norm. There are some cool, open- sounding grooves that can be achieved by this sound. As for the size, I have been using a 20" bass drum for a number of years because I like its focus and punch. It really serves the style well. The depth I prefer is 18", although a 16" would suffice.

Class Notes: _____

_____

_____

_____

_____

_____

Buried or Alive?

With all this talk about the importance of the bass-drum tuning, we must also talk about how to execute the right sound. This leads us to the inevitable question of technique. Just as we discussed earlier, about "rimshot or not" on the snare, "buried or alive" refers to the bass-drum beater, and whether to leave it on the head—commonly referred to as "buried"—or pull it off the head and keep the head 'alive' or "open." In my opinion, tuning and style are the deciding factors in determining the right approach. Also, the amount of velocity one gets from the bass-drum sound, the more solid it is.

As we discussed in the section on the bass-drum sound, the "dry," "punchy" sound is accepted as the most common. To achieve this, playing with the heel up on the ball of the foot and leaving the beater on the head provides a solid attack and punch, and a more definitive, articulate, and consistent sound. Here's how to achieve this sound.

Begin with the beater on the head, heel up slightly. IN ONE MOTION, push off the head, lift the leg from the knee, and then follow through back into the bass drum, "sticking" the beater into the head. The weight of the leg combined with the velocity will create a nice fat, "thump" sound. Be sure not to "float" your leg in the air for any length of time, especially to take the beater off of the head. The higher you lift your leg, the more velocity, and the more sound you will get. A lesser amount of lift creates a lighter sound.

A great way to practice this is on the floor, to feel the leg lift and the solid contact. Feel the foot grounded on the floor, on the ball of the foot, and practice pushing off the floor and letting the leg just fall into the floor again to the ball of the foot. It's a "push off" type of feeling. When you do this for a while, return to the pedal, start with the beater on the head and recreate the same feeling.

Remember this analogy: Foot is to floor, as beater is to bass-drum head.

The Rest of the Kit

The tom-toms I generally use for this style are smaller, featuring 10" and 12" rack toms and a 14" floor tom with legs. The smaller drums are easier to tune, and the 14" in particular can be tuned low and still maintain tone and clarity. The truly "old-school" sound would be one rack tom, probably a 12" or 13", and one floor tom, probably a 16", although 14" floor toms were prevalent.

For drumheads, I prefer Remo-Coated Emporers for a classic sound, or Clear Pinstripes for a more contemporary sound and punch. On the bass drum, I use the versatile Remo Powersonic, with its removeable muffle pad which snaps on the head. Clear or coated works fine for me.

As for the cymbals, my Zildjian setup includes 13" Mastersound hi-hats for a tighter, quicker sound, a 21" K Prototype ride cymbal that can also be crashed with a very dry, distinctive bell. The crashes are all dark K's, including 17", 16", and 14" crashes, and 10" and 12" prototype splashes.

Class Notes: _____

_____

_____

_____

_____

_____

_____

CHAPTER 1:
Early R&B Roots

New Orleans R&B

It is widely recognized that the term "Rhythm and Blues" was coined in 1947 by Jerry Winkler at Billboard Magazine and later, brought it with him when he went on to Atlantic Records. Atlantic became the preeminent label in the R&B field. In the 1950s, Rhythm & Blues music evolved as a derivative of New Orleans styles, Blues, Gospel and Early Swing. This would explain why the early R&B classics had a "shuffle" or "swing" feel. An early example of the style is the Ray Charles classic *I've Got a Woman*. Recorded in 1954, its strong swing, "two-beat" groove would anoint Ray Charles as one of the creators of this genre. This strong, distinct style was cultivated from New Orleans, based on the swinging piano style first made famous by the great Professor Longhair. In the late 1950s, the Fats Domino tune *I'm Walkin'* was another landmark in the progression of Rhythm & Blues, and one of the leading drummers in New Orleans who played on many of these records was the legendary Earl Palmer. He was one of the first drummers to bring the roots of the "Second Line" March rhythm into popular music during this period.

This is highlighted in our first example. The snare "caters" are swung, and the accents create a "two-beat" feel. The fourth bar of the pattern uses a syncopated sixteenth-note accent turnaround between the snare and the bass. The B-section groove goes to the hi-hat, keeping the accent on the snare in the "two-beat" feel, while the bass drum gets more syncopated, following the bass guitar part. Then, we move the same part to the ride cymbal, with upbeats on the hi-hat.

Strollin'
CD Track #1

Example No. 1: Strollin'

Chart Roadmap: A (2x), B, Repeated

The Soul Shuffle

In the early 1960s, many of the grooves were still based on the "shuffle/swing" feel, but were slowed down a bit, which created more opportunity for interplay. This was never more evident than in the classic James Brown track *Doin' it to Death*.

In the 1950s and 1960s, the electrification of the rhythm section, namely the electric bass with the Fender Precision Bass in 1951, was a landmark development. The replacement of the acoustic double bass with the electric bass anchored the R&B rhythm section. The electrification of the rhythm section transformed the role of the guitar from a lead voice to a more supportive role. Hence, the term "rhythm guitar" became popularized. These two instruments weaved around the solid backdrop of the drum groove.

In this example, the guitar creates the shuffle feel with a quarter-note triplet rhythmic feel. The bass player plays a flowing triplet bass line over the top. The drum part dances between both parts, uniting the rhythm section.

The Shuffle Soufflé
CD Track #2

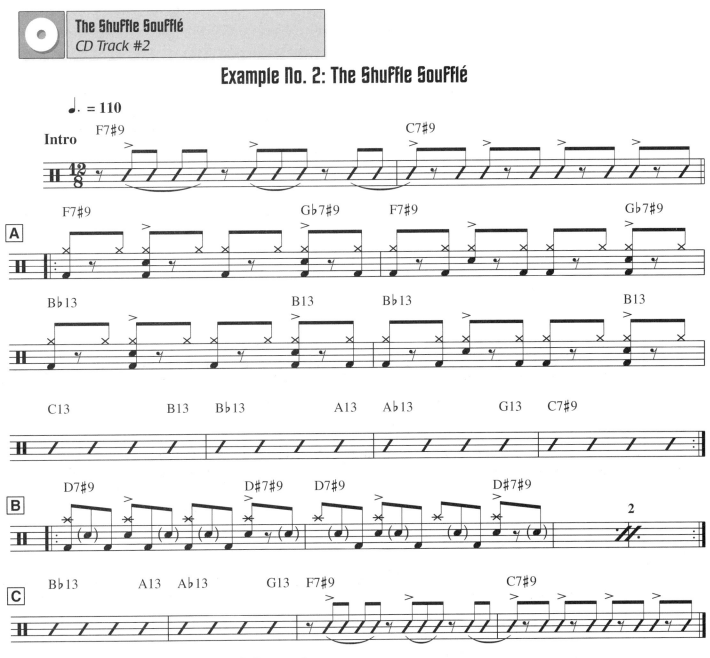

Example No. 2: The Shuffle Soufflé

Chart Roadmap: Intro, A (2x), B (2x), C, Repeated

CHAPTER 2:
The Grooves of Motown
[Medium Tempo Shuffle, Two-Beat Shuffle, Classic Motown]

Taking the cue from the Roots R&B from New Orleans, Berry Gordy's Motown Records empire based in Detroit began to take the shuffle into a more popular dance feel by making it faster, appealing to a younger audience. This soul was strongly rhythmic, and was also continually influenced by Gospel music. The Motown Sound often includes hand clapping, a powerful bass line, violins, bells and more elaborate orchestrations. Motown's house band backed up artists such as Marvin Gaye, The Temptations, Smokey Robinson & the Miracles, Gladys Knight & the Pips, Martha Reeves & the Vandellas, The Marvelettes, Mary Wells, Diana Ross & the Supremes, The Jackson 5, The Four Tops and Stevie Wonder. The heart of Motown was the strong songwriters, which included Holland-Dozier-Holland, Norman Whitfield, Barrett Strong, and Smokey Robinson. The rhythm-section team of Benny Benjamin and "Pistol" Allen on drums, and James Jamerson on bass, became known as "the Funk Brothers."

There are three essential Motown feels which are critical to learn because of their use in a variety of songs. The first example is a medium shuffle, and you can hear the New Orleans influence in the feel. The A-section is the classic Motown shuffle, and the B-section switches to a quarter-note pulse for a few bars to build the intensity, which then returns to the shuffle hi-hat part.

> **Hot Flashes**
> *CD Track #3*

Example No. 3: Hot Flashes

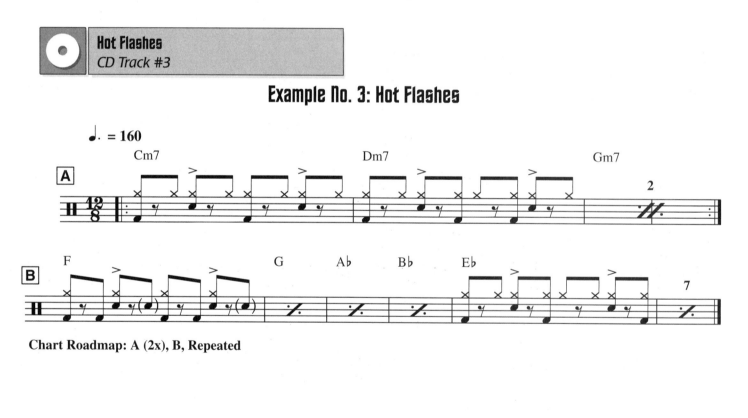

Chart Roadmap: A (2x), B, Repeated

Class Notes: _____

_____

_____

The next Motown shuffle is faster, and it's felt in a fast "2." The beginning rides the floor tom, emphasizing the rhythm of the song, then returns to the hi-hat with a quarter-note pulse. The B-section maintains the groove, except it is played on the ride cymbal over quarter notes on the hi-hat. The legendary "Motown Review," which made its way around the country by bus, brought this great music to the teenagers in the dance halls.

Can't Hold Back
CD Track #4

Example No. 4: Can't Hold Back

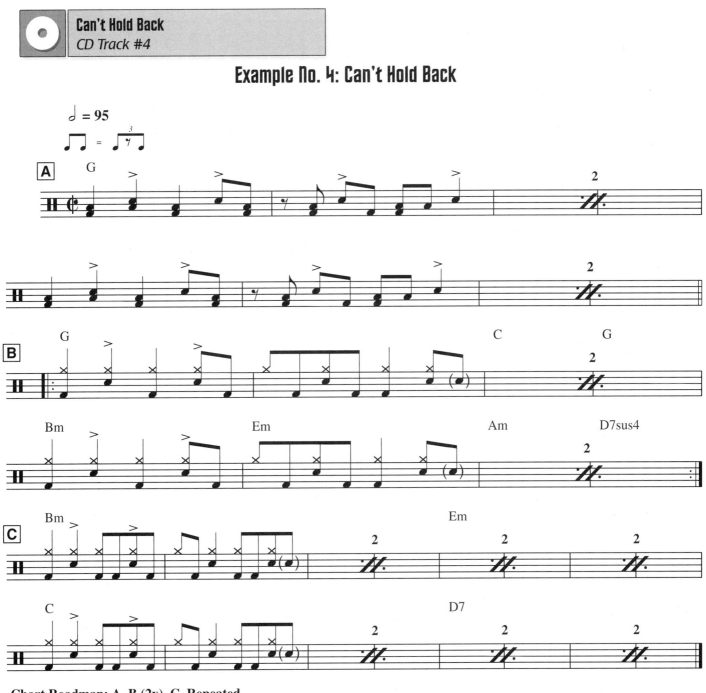

Chart Roadmap: A, B (2x), C, Repeated

Class Notes: _____

_____

_____

Finally, we come to the classic Motown beat that, strangely, many drummers have heard, but when asked to play it, can't recall how it goes. It was the beat that made the "Motown Sound" popular throughout the world. A simple, yet driving feel with quarter notes on the snare, and a bass drum rhythm that mixes up "downbeats" and "upbeats" completes the rhythmic contrast. Note the classic six-stroke roll fill going into A, and again going back to the verse.

Motorin'
CD Track #5

Example No. 5: Motorin'

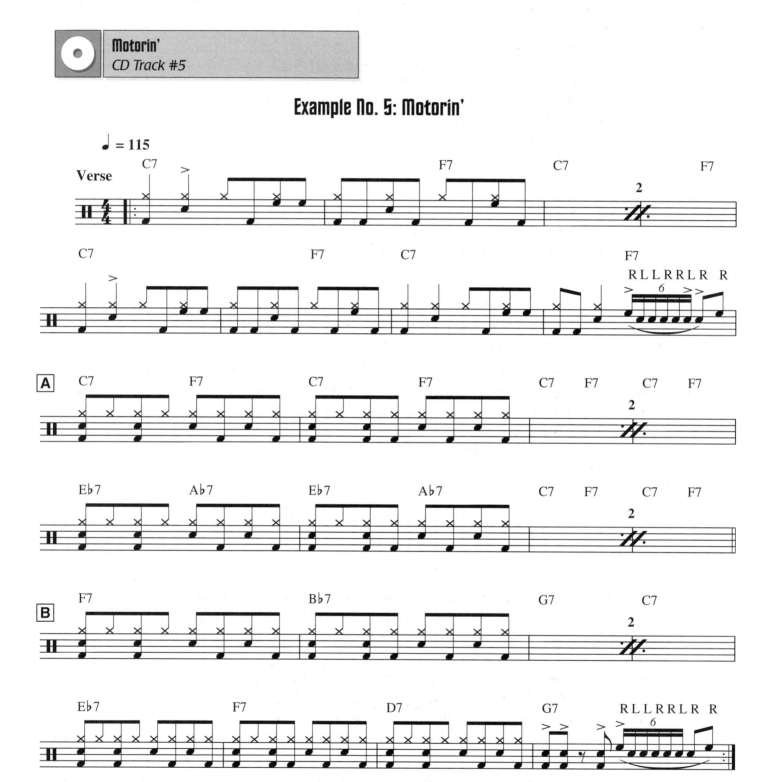

Chart Roadmap: Verse, A, B, Repeated

So, there you have the three main grooves of Motown. I suggest you buy the box-set compilation *Hitsville USA: The Motown Singles Collection 1959–1971*. In this set are all of the most popular Motown songs to learn, so that you'll know which groove goes with what song. It'll be a challenge, but I guarantee you will play at least fifteen of these songs at some point if you become a working drummer "on the circuit."

CHAPTER 3:
Essential R&B/Soul

While Motown was building in its empire in Detroit, the original form of Rhythm & Blues created in the south was evolving into a more complex sound. The blues vocals were mixed with a "grittier" rhythm section, which used more syncopated rhythms, orchestrated horn sections, and a more powerful sound. Lyrically, the music became a commentary on social issues, more conscious of its role in society, particularly in the neighborhoods of young urban America. The music was speaking to a new generation. Feelings of oppression were manifesting themselves into music that was filled with passion, pride, and, yes, soul. "Soul Music" was an expression of these feelings, and James Brown was its spiritual leader, the "Godfather of Soul." The music that Brown created was often improvised; the grooves were then refined by a great rhythm section including the drummers Clyde Stubblefield and John "Jabo" Starks. Horn parts and guitar riffs were carefully placed to complement the syncopation created by the drummers and the bass line.

The Fatback Beat

One very unique and different groove came out of this era that is still being utilized in many different ways in today's music. The "Fatback Beat" was played on many records, and was the groove of choice on many of James Brown's popular tracks, including *Cold Sweat* and *Mother Popcorn*. This two-bar groove is recognized by the snare "turnaround" on the & of 4 in the first bar, with no bass drum on 1 of the second bar. This syncopated part set in motion a series of rhythmic syncopations complemented by the bass and guitar player, allowing them to find their spots, filling in the holes. The result was a landmark groove, becoming a standard feel often imitated and recreated by countless groups.

This track uses the "Fatback Beat" with some variations in the bridge section, displacing the snare in other locations. Learning this style of groove will lay the foundation to do more complex beat-displaced grooves in the upcoming sections.

R U B'n Fun K
CD Track #6

Example No. 6: R U B'n Fun K?

Chart Roadmap: A (4x), B (2x), C (2x), Repeated, D

Swingin' Soul

Being an offshoot of the early R&B tree, there is also an element of swing to many soul grooves. These grooves laid the foundation to many sub-genres that followed, including Hip Hop, New Jack Swing, and Neo-Soul. The sixteenths are "swung" with a jazz lilt which permeates the music and creates an easy, laid-back groove, yet has a lot of intensity. The ghost notes create interesting interplay between the hi-hat and snare, similar to Jazz. The part in the bridge section explores more interplay, with an eighth-note feel on the hi-hat, and syncopation between the snare and bass drums to complement the guitar part.

In order to make the sixteenth notes swing, delay them just a bit and put a little more "spread" between the notes.

Swingin' Soul
CD Track #7

Example No. 7: Swingin' Soul

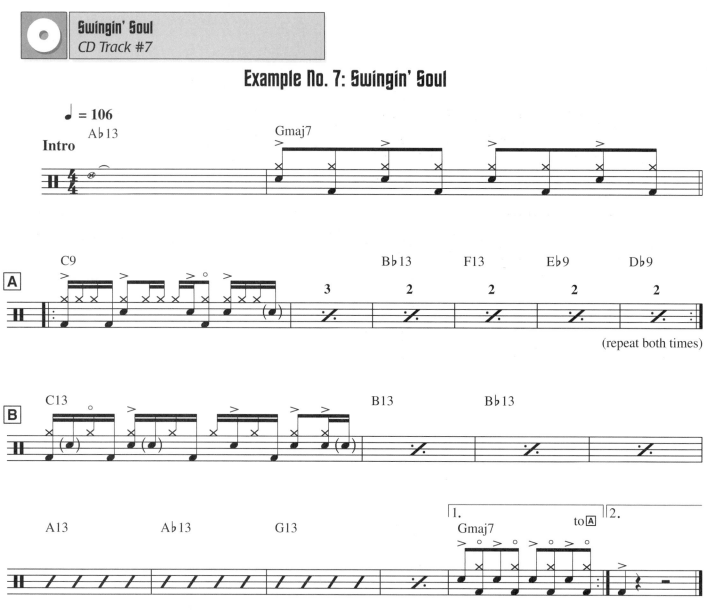

(repeat both times)

Chart Roadmap: Intro, A (2x), B, Repeated

Funky Stuff

Many Essential R&B/Soul grooves of this period were punctuated by syncopated sixteenth-note snare accents and a variety of ghost-note placements. In this final example of Essential R&B/Soul, I've created some examples of how these various movements make a groove percolate with interest, while keeping it danceable, not too busy, and connected to the entire rhythm section. The A-section utilizes a sixteenth-note pattern on the hi-hat with one hand, while the other creates interesting ghosting colorations on the snare drum. There are variations in the B-section that will shift the timing to different parts of the beat. The feel is straight sixteenth notes. Be careful not to swing this one.

Example No. 8: Funky Stuff

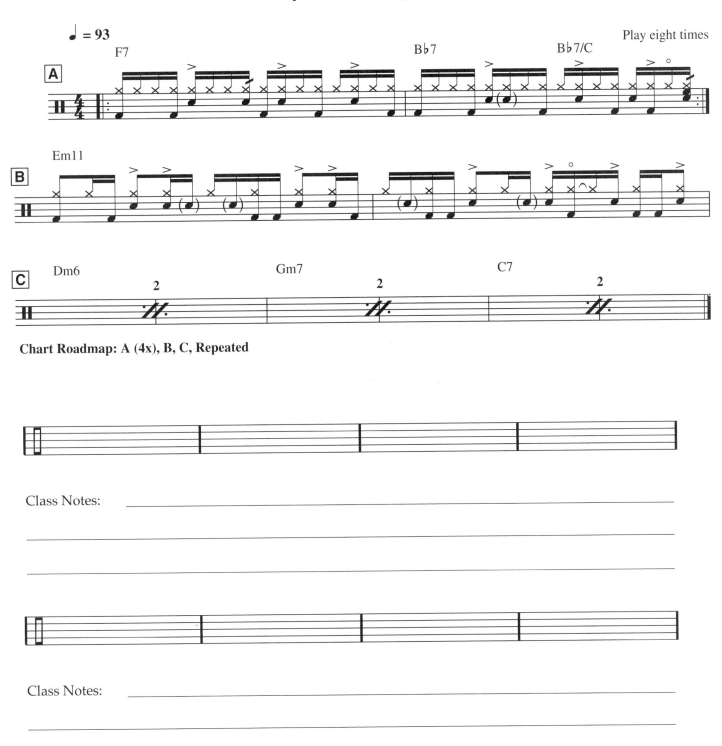

Chart Roadmap: A (4x), B, C, Repeated

Class Notes: _____

_____

_____

Class Notes: _____

_____

_____

Class Notes: _____

_____

_____

Class Notes: _____

_____

_____

Class Notes: _____

_____

_____

Class Notes: _____

_____

_____

Class Notes: _____

_____

_____

CHAPTER 4:
Essential Funk

Now we will shift gears into the realm of Funk. The following grooves and concepts are what I would consider essential to learn, because they laid the groundwork for much of today's contemporary Funk sound. They also incorporate elements from previous groove genres, combining solid pocket playing with interesting ghost note ideas and accent placement, with a touch of linear phrasing thrown in for good measure.

I will try to help define certain terms and provide musical context for you to experience the feeling of how these grooves should be played. Once you have performed these with the tracks, your future performances will come from a more informed perspective.

The Funk Bands

The 70s gave birth to the Funk Band Era. Some of the drummers and those bands included Diamond from the Ohio Players, Jerome "Sugarfoot" Brailey and Tiki Fulwood from Parliament/Funkadelic, Tony Thompson from Chic, Larry Blackmon from Cameo, Jonathan Moffet with Michael Jackson (Live), Michael Beard of the Bar Kays, and many others. All of these drummers personified Funk drumming, highlighting the bass drum as the lead voice, using more syncopated sixteenth-note rhythms which gave the groove more "punch," and created rhythmic interest for the bass player to follow, or "lock" into.

The Lock and the Bass Player

No, it's not a new MTV *reality* show! Although this is primarily a drummer's book, I want to "give the bass player some." The *reality* of Funk music is that many of the songs were written around a "bass line," which became "hooks," or very recognizable parts of the song, sometimes even more than the melody or lyric. The first step in this direction came from bassist Larry Graham with the group Sly & The Family Stone. He was an innovator, who pioneered the Funk technique of "slapping and popping," which gave the music a very percussive feel, allowing drummer Greg Errico to play more simplified grooves, as evidenced on the track *Thank You Falletinme Be Myself Again*. So, the "lock" started to be the accepted practice of creating music "from the bottom up" in this style.

Many other notable bass players began to follow suit, including Louis "Thunder Thumbs" Johnson from The Brothers Johnson, "Bootsy" Collins (who also played with James Brown), and Bernard Edwards of Chic, who created the memorable bass line for the song *Good Times*, which later became the hook for the first crossover rap song *Rapper's Delight* by the Sugarhill Gang. These players defined a musical culture and genre with creativity. Also, bass lines were now being played using synthesizers, creating a new sound and direction for Funk. One of the leaders in synthesized bass playing was Bernie Worrell from Parliament/Funkadelic. This contrast of rhythmic-flavored bass lines with simple, direct drum grooves allowed the two instruments to merge into one voice, creating what became known as a "pocket" of groove.

The Pocket

The "pocket" is a term musicians began to use for a great groove, like when you place something in your pocket so it is *secure, doesn't move, and won't get lost.* What better way to describe a groove! It's a feeling of the groove "sitting" and not rushing, while presenting an attitude of "danceability" and steadiness. However, it does not necessarily mean "laid back." This is the element that people latch onto: the infectious and repetitious groove of the rhythm section. When playing along with these grooves, try not to play any fills. Simply lock it down with the bass player. You have to feel the placement of the bass drum and the bass player in the rhythm section. Many people have tried to describe what a "pocket" is and what it means.

The way I can describe it is by telling you what it *isn't*, as well as what it *is:*

- It *isn't* perfect metronomic time.
- It's the space *between* the notes; a "settled," "unhurried" groove that works at any tempo.
- It's a groove that is "breathing" and alive, not "stiff" and robotic.
- It's *not* playing "behind the beat"; that's dragging.
- It's not a busy groove.

Here are some examples of how to create the lock with a rhythmic bass line, and a simple, complementary drum part. The bass-drum part is helping to create that unified sound. Although these may seem like simplistic eighth-note grooves, making them feel right in "the pocket" is difficult, while allowing time for the bass player to "slap and pop" inside the groove.

Each of the patterns in Examples 9–11 graduate in difficulty, adding bass-drum variations while maintaining the "lock" with the bass player. Add any of the Groove Variations from p. 7 on top of these.

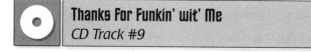

Thanks For Funkin' wit' Me
CD Track #9

Example No. 9: Thanks For Funkin' wit' Me

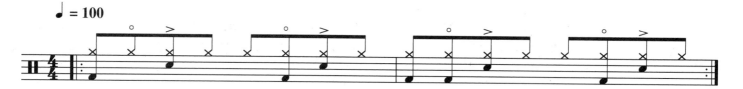

Variation 1 on Thanks For Funkin' wit' Me
CD Track #10

Example No. 10: Variation 1 on Thanks For Funkin' wit' Me

Example No. 11: Variation 2 on Thanks For Funkin' wit' Me

This groove focuses on "double sixteenth" execution on the bass drum. Be sure to articulate each note on the bass drum, and not "slide" over the first sixteenth. On the variations, I fill in with some "ghosting" ideas, while the bass drum line becomes more syncopated.

Example No. 12: Don't Stop the Funk

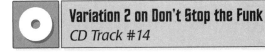

Example No. 13: Variation 1 on Don't Stop the Funk

Example No. 14: Variation 2 on Don't Stop the Funk

A two-bar phrase, this classic groove is what I affectionately call the "funk clave," very usable in many settings. These variations feature some "displaced snare" accents for extra flavor, again, coinciding with the bass line phrase, concluding with the re-introduction of the "fatback" beat from the previous section.

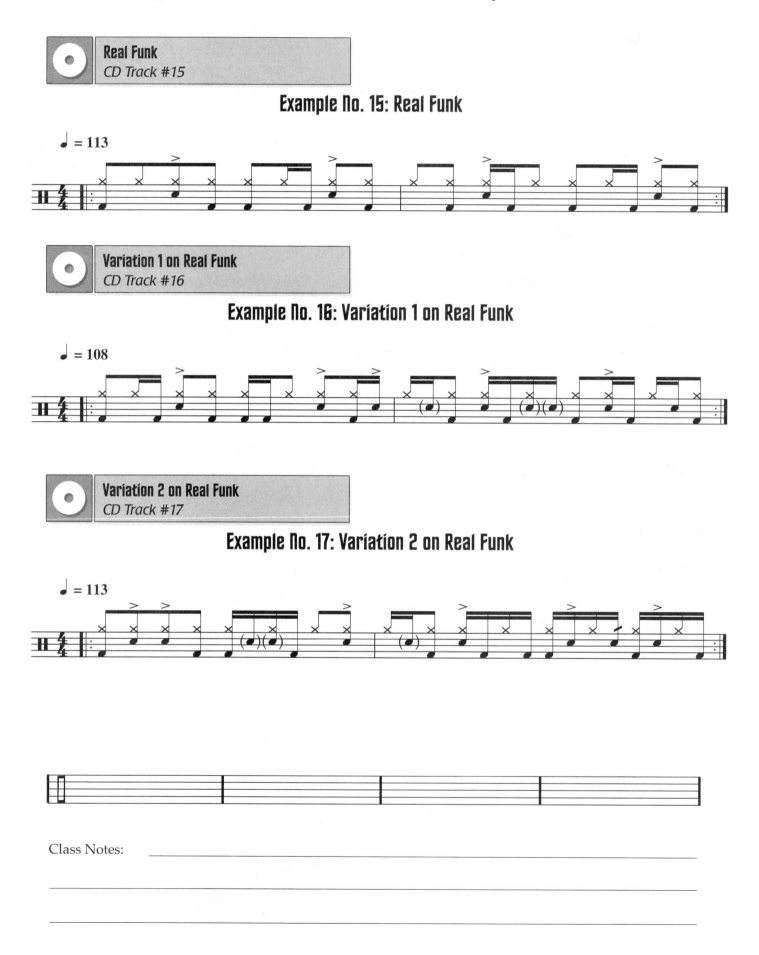

Real Funk
CD Track #15

Example No. 15: Real Funk

Variation 1 on Real Funk
CD Track #16

Example No. 16: Variation 1 on Real Funk

Variation 2 on Real Funk
CD Track #17

Example No. 17: Variation 2 on Real Funk

Class Notes: _____

_____

_____

Now we can begin to shift the phrasing of these grooves, creating some displacement in the bass- drum part. By not starting with the bass on 1, you can immediately feel the "shiftiness" that takes place, which sets off a chain reaction that allows for some interesting ghost-note ideas to follow around the bass line. These should provide a fun challenge both from a displacement and ghost- note standpoint.

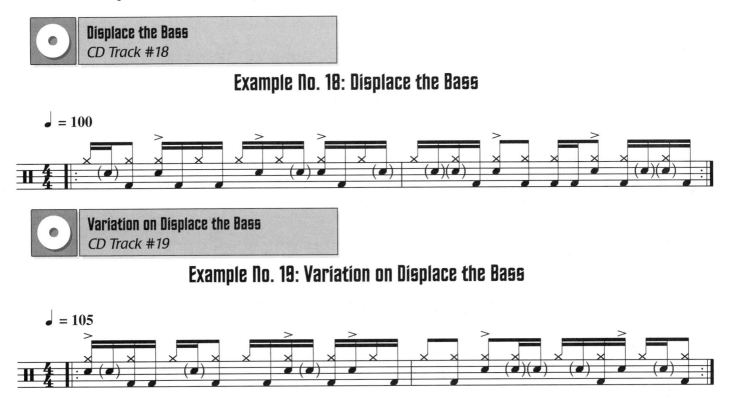

Displace the Bass
CD Track #18

Example No. 18: Displace the Bass

Variation on Displace the Bass
CD Track #19

Example No. 19: Variation on Displace the Bass

Linear Funk

Eventually, more "technically proficient" players began playing a new form of Funk. Expanding on the concepts of the early James Brown bands, groups began adding more musical complexities. Groups like Tower of Power, with the rhythm section of drummer David Garibaldi and bassist Rocco Prestia, created a "West Coast" sound that reintroduced the busier "ghost-note" approach to the drumming world, with a nod to Clyde Stubblefield, but with a bit more independent voicings being orchestrated on the drumkit. This approach became known as "linear" drumming, which simply means, the drum part became more of a music "line." In essence, it was the hi-hat voice that began to play more than just eighth notes. Harvey Mason did the same with Herbie Hancock's *Chameleon*, and Mike Clark with the Fusion/Funk of *Actual Proof*.

DisFunktion is a piece that I wrote to provide a vehicle to play in the "linear" style of funk. It's an example of how linear drumming can be used to create interesting parts based around the concept of using various "diddle" stickings, including the Inverted Paradiddle, and Paradiddle-Diddle.

The A-section part was created based on the bass-drum rhythm that is being orchestrated. I tried to create an independent sounding line, and this pattern made sense with the music. That should always be your goal. Be sure to not go crazy with independent patterns as they tend to sound too busy.

If you were to isolate the right and left hand parts, the diddle pattern for the A-section is as follows:

Example No. 20: Linear Diddle Pattern No. 1 (not on CD)

The B-section diddle pattern is based on the paradiddle-diddle as follows:

Example No. 21: Linear Diddle Pattern No. 2 (not on CD)

DisFunktion
CD Track #20

Example No. 22: DisFunktion

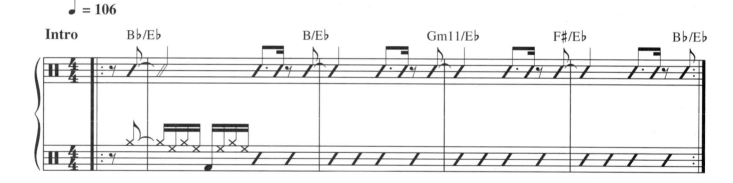

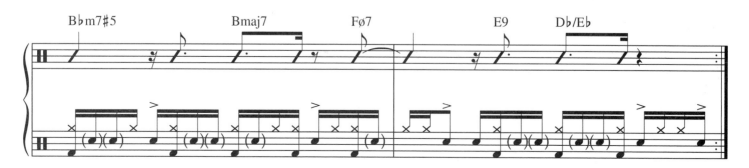

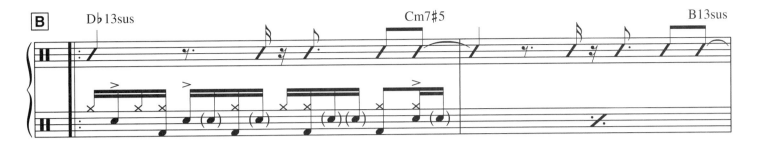

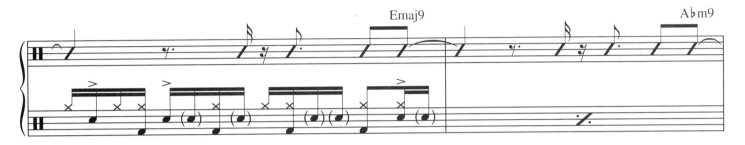

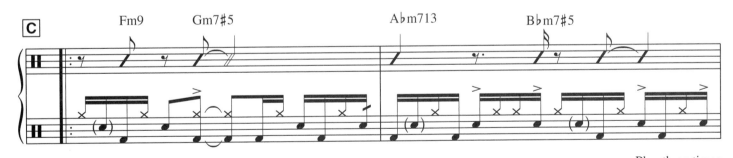

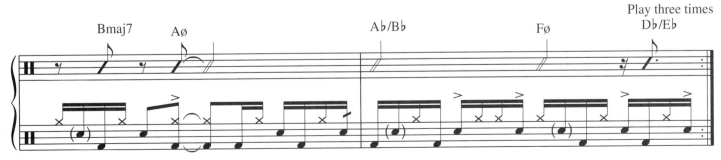

Chart Roadmap: A (2x), B (2x), Repeated, C (3x)

CHAPTER 5:
Go-Go, Hip Hop and New Jack Swing Styles

Originating in Washington DC in the 1980s, the "Go-Go" sound is a medium-tempo Funk groove that "swings" the sixteenth note and uses contrapuntal percussion to add rhythmic flavor. The Go-Go group E.U. had a big hit with *Da' Butt* in the late 80s. Later, under the new label of "New Jack Swing," groups like GUY, New Edition (later known as Bell Biv Devoe), and Boyz II Men, popularized the style. The 80s sound is defined by this genre of Funk. However, as we know, everything is based on what has come before it musically, so you will hear a lot of similarities to the "Swingin' Soul" groove in the earlier part of this book.

In the 90s, the styles began to merge, and the lines between Hip Hop, R&B and New Jack Swing became blurred. The swing permeated every musical form, and producers were using these New Jack Swing grooves with Urban R&B artists. Mary J. Blige, the queen of Hip-Hop Soul, brought this style to the forefront. Today, "Neo-Soul," or new soul sound, is the leading style in R&B, with artists merging an old-school vocal style with today's production. Today, such artists as The Roots, Erykah Badu, Mary J. Blige, John Legend, Alicia Keyes, and Soulive are at the forefront of this new genre.

Another form of R&B/Funk on the rise is Contemporary Gospel music. It has also had a huge influence on music, with Gospel chord progressions and grooves crossing over into the R&B world. Gospel artists such as John P. Kee, Kirk Franklin, Fred Hammond, Yolanda Adams, Mary Mary, Kim Burrell and others have created a genre that is as musically complex as it is inspiring. A fusion of Jazz, Hip Hop, R&B, and Blues, Gospel music is becoming a breeding ground for great rhythm sections. To play this style completely, one needs to work on interpreting the "swing sixteenth-note" bass-drum patterns. Then, once this is executed, various ghost-note colorations can be added to texture the groove with subtle rhythmic interest.

The examples provided are a cross section of styles that reflect the trends in today's R&B; each are unique, with there own tempo and feel. Listen to some of the artists and music mentioned and you will see the cross pollination from one sub-style to the next.

This is a medium-tempo groove that focuses on swinging two sixteenth-note bass-drum rhythms together in a couple of different places. There are two grooves, with the A-groove being the basic Hip-Hop Swing groove, and the B-groove a more broken-up linear pattern, which is considered to be *the* Go-Go beat. Play it on the bell. Practice both separately, then alternate between the two grooves.

Hip Hop/Go-Go
CD Track #21

Example No. 23: Hip Hop/Go-Go

Form: A-groove for 16 bars.
B-groove for 16 bars.

The New Jack/Philly/Gospel style swing is a little faster, "jazzier," with more ghosting, and at times, a busier bass drum. With that in mind, move to the ride cymbal and try playing a standard "Jazz ride" pattern with the hi-hat on 2 & 4 over the top of these grooves. This approach can be very useful in a Jazz/Funk application.

New Jack/Philly/Gospel Swing
CD Track #22

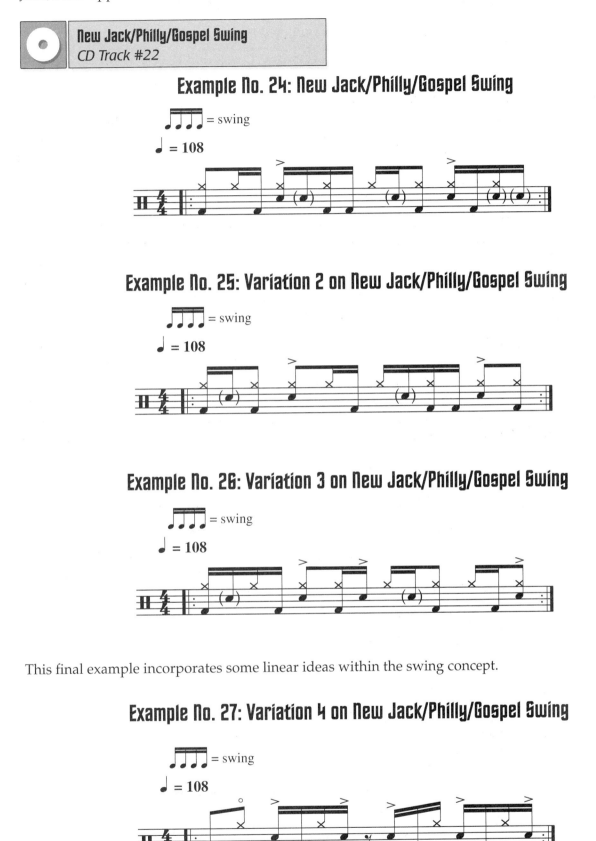

Example No. 24: New Jack/Philly/Gospel Swing

Example No. 25: Variation 2 on New Jack/Philly/Gospel Swing

Example No. 26: Variation 3 on New Jack/Philly/Gospel Swing

This final example incorporates some linear ideas within the swing concept.

Example No. 27: Variation 4 on New Jack/Philly/Gospel Swing

In summary, today's R&B/Funk styles, whether it's Pop, Neo Soul, Hip Hop, or Gospel, are all connected by the same thread, and that is the history of groove music that preceded them. What's old is new again, with many new drummers taking the stage that have taken this style of drumming to new heights. Dennis Chambers, Teddy Campbell, Zoro, Gerald Heyward and many others are bringing Funk drumming to a new audience, while creating incredible variations of grooves created by the masters from yesterday.

DISCOGRAPHY

Here is a discography of some great compilations where you will find these classic recordings.

- *Atlantic Rhythm & Blues:* 1947–1974 (WEA 81293) 8-CD box set
- Brown, James. *20 All-Time Greatest Hits!* (Polygram 511326)
- Charles, Ray. *The Very Best of Ray Charles* (Rhino 79822)
- Franklin, Aretha. *The Very Best of Aretha Franklin, Vol. 1* (Rhino 71598)
- Hitsville USA. *The Motown Singles Collection, 1959–1971* (Motown 6312) 4-CD box set
- Jordan, Louis. *The Best of Louis Jordan* (MCA 4079)
- Parliament. *Give up the Funk: Best of Parliament* (Mercury 526995)
- R&B Box, The. *30 Years of Rhythm and Blues* (Rhino 71806) 6-CD box set
- WOW Gospel compilations: Various years from 2000 to now.

Here is just a sample of a few classic R&B/Funk singles to check out. You can easily find them on the internet, in many CD compilations or on iTunes.

Everyday People	Sly & The Family Stone
Family Affair	Sly & The Family Stone
Cold Sweat	James Brown
What's Going on?	Marvin Gaye
Let's Stay Together	Al Green
Will It Go 'round in Circles?	Billy Preston
Superstition	Stevie Wonder
Higher Ground	Stevie Wonder
Do I Do	Stevie Wonder
Boogie on Reggae Woman	Stevie Wonder
Can't Get Enough of Your Love, Babe	Barry White
You're the First, the Last, My Everything	Barry White
Theme from "Shaft"	Isaac Hayes
Walking in Rhythm	The Blackbyrds
Rock Creek Park	The Blackbyrds
Lady Marmalade	LaBelle
Got to Give It up	Marvin Gaye
(Every Time I Turn Around) Back in Love Again	L.T.D.
Shinin' Star	Earth, Wind & Fire
Let's Groove	Earth, Wind & Fire
Brick House	The Commodores
Got to Be Real	Cheryl Lynn
The Pride	The Isley Brothers
Do You Love What You Feel?	Rufus & Chaka Khan
Slave	Slide
Stomp!	Brothers Johnson
Cissy Strut	The Meters
Rock Steady	The Whispers

It's a Love Thing .... The Whispers

Somebody Else's Guy ....Jocelyn Brown

Lady Marmalade .... LaBelle

Funkin' for Jamaica .... Tom Browne

Love Rollercoaster ....Ohio Players

Pick up the Pieces .... Average White Band

Burn Rubber (Why You Wanna Hurt Me?) .... The Gap Band

Brick.. Dazz

The Breaks .... Kurtis Blow

Good Times .... Chic

Soup for One .... Chic

777-9311...The Time

Sexy Dancer... Prince

Give up the Funk (Tear the Roof off the Sucker) .... Parliament

One Nation under a Groove .... Funkadelic

(Not Just) Knee Deep ....Funkadelic

Strange .... Cameo

Before I Let Go ....Frankie Beverley & Maze

Always and Forever .... Heatwave

Square Biz ....Teena Marie

Can't You See?.. Tower of Power

Soul Vaccination .... Tower of Power

Real Love ....Mary J. Blige

Da' Butt...E.U.

Groove Me ....Guy

Rub You the Right Way.. Johnny Gil

My Prerogative .... Bobby Brown

Motown/Philly...Boyz II Men

Gonna Make You Sweat................................... C&C Music Factory

Like I Love You .... Justin Timberlake

Don't Sweat the Technique .... Eric B. & Rakim

Boyfriend ....Me 'Shell NdegéOcello

He Can Handle It..Kirk Franklin

I'll Keep Holdin' on..Kim Burrell

RECOMMENDED READINGS

Here are some books that should provide some great insight on R&B music:

- Bogdanov, Vladimir. *All Music Guide to Soul: The Definitive Guide to R&B and Soul.* Backbeat Books, 2003.
- Broven John. *Rhythm and Blues in New Orleans.* Pelican Publishing Company, 1983.
- Pavlow, "Big" Al. *Big Al Pavlow's the R and B Book: A Disc-History of Rhythm & Blues.* Music House Publishing, 1983.
- White, Adam. *The Billboard Book of Number One Rhythm & Blues Hits.* Billboard Books, 1993.

thecollective
Contemporary Styles Series

BOOKS WITH CDs

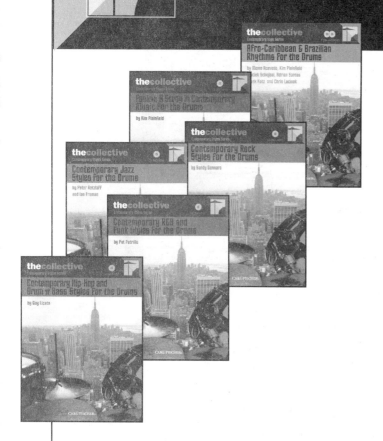

The material in The Collective Contemporary Styles Series represents many years of work on the part of many talented Collective faculty members, who have the experience of playing and teaching these styles to literally thousands of young rhythm-section musicians over the last thirty years. This series is the fruit of their labor and talent with the information presented in a manner that is easy to grasp.

CO1 **Afro-Caribean & Brazilian Rhythms for the Drums**
    By Memo Acevedo, Frank Katz, Chris Lacinak, Kim Plainfield, Adrian Santos, and Maciek Schijbal

CO2 **Afro-Caribean & Brazilian Rhythms for the Bass**
    By Lincoln Goines, Steve Marks, Nilson Matta, Irio O'Farill and Leo Traversa

CO3 **Fusion: A Study in Contemporary Music for the Drums**
    By Kim Plainfield

CO4 **Fusion: A Study in Contemporary Music for the Bass**
    By Leo Traversa

CO5 **Contemporary Rock Styles for the Drums**
    By Sandy Gennaro

CO6 **Contemporary Rock Styles for the Bass**
    By Gary Kelly

CO7 **Contemporary Jazz Styles for the Drums**
    By Ian Froman and Peter Retzlaff

CO8 **Contemporary Jazz Styles for the Bass**
    By Joe Fitzgerald and Hilliard Greene

CO9 **The Roots of Groove: R&B/Soul & Contemporary R&B and Funk Styles for the Drums**
    By Pat Petrillo

CO10 **Contemporary R&B and Funk Styles for the Bass**
    By Frank Gravis and Steve Marks

CO11 **Contemporary Hip Hop and Drum 'n' Bass Styles for the Drums**
    By Guy Licata

CO12 **Contemporary Hip Hop and Drum 'n' Bass Styles for the Bass**
    By John Davis

CARL FISCHER
MUSIC

Must Have International Grooves

Brazilian Rhythms for the Drumset
Bossa Nova and Samba
Henrique C. De Almeida

This book offers the reader an in depth look at Bossa Nova and Samba rhythms including the cultural origins, applications and role in Brazilian society. Almeida clearly gives drummers the tools that they need to incorporate these styles and a myriad of their variants into their own drumset technique, adding a new scope to their sound while achieving an authentic Brazilian feel.

DRM119 – Book w/2CDs
CD2 "Play Along" featuring the Brazilian Jazz Project

★★★★✦
Modern Drummer

Also Recommended...
ABCs of Brazilian Percussion
Ney Rosauro
DRM118 – Book w/DVD

Afro-Caribbean & Brazilian Rhythms for the Drumset
Drummers Collective
One of the most detailed books on the subject based on the curriculum of the famed Drummers Collective in New York City.
CO1 – Book w/2CDs – $24.95

Vodou Drumset
James Armstrong/ Travis Knepper
Drumset applications for traditional Afro-Hatian rhythms that include Ibo, Nago, and Yanvalou.
DRM103 – Book w/CD

Best Selling Drumset Books
JAZZ • FUNK • FUSION

Take It to the Street

A Study in New Orleans Street Beats and Second-line Rhythms as Applied to Funk
Stanton Moore

In this book, the reader will learn about the history of street beats, second-line, and the Mardi Gras Indians as well as the importance of clave to New Orleans drumming. The reader will also learn how to put a New Orleans spin on traditional rhythms like mambo, guaguanco, shuffle, and samba. Stanton teaches how to play between the cracks, bring more inflection and variation to a groove, and how to incorporate a bit of Crescent City flavor into linear playing. Accompanying CD includes performances by the Dirty Dozen, George Porter, and Ivan Neville.

Take It to the Street (Moore) - DRM115 – Book w/CD

Musical Time - Ed Soph

Distinguished drummer Ed Soph, known for his mastery of technique and musicality, brings you a book and CD that help drummers become more comfortable with time. The book features ideas on set-up, coordination studies, playing the shuffle, non-repetitive ride patterns, dynamic balance and much more! The included CD brings the user performances by a fantastic trio as well as extended play-along tracks in various tempos.

DRM113 – Book w/CD

Exercises for Natural Playing – Dave Weckl

Based on the award-winning *A Natural Evolution* DVD series, *Exercises for Natural Playing* (book and CD) offers the reader exciting new exercises and concepts not covered in the DVDs, as well as material complementary to the series. Dave provides written details, photos, and performance examples on the CD that will help players evolve their technique naturally. Sure to be a great resource for al drummers!

Weckl provides key insight into:
• Hand positioning
• The Moeller Technique
• Bass drum pedal work
• Playing without losing time
• Time and Motion
DRM110 – Book w/CD

Playing with Drum Loops – Donny Gruendler

In this book, drummers will get the tools they need to improve their musicianship and add the use of loops to their repertoire to make them a complete package. DJs and Electronica artists will find their work more musical and will be able to add intricate layers to their sound through the use of this book. Also perfect for home recording enthusiasts!
DRM120 – Book w/2 CDs

Advanced Funk Studies

by Rick Latham

Rick Latham's first drum book, *Advanced Funk Studies*, is one of the definitive books for the contemporary drummer Now again available, in a new edition that includes a two-CD set, this standard in the field is a compilation of all the drumming techniques used in Funk and Fusion Music The book includes transcriptions by the author of excerpts from many celebrated recordings by drummers such as Steve Gladd, David Garibaldi, Harvey Mason, Peter Erskine and many others, as well as specially constructed solos by the author The two CD set contains recordings of all the patterns; transcriptions and solos as performed by author, Rick Latham This is a book that belongs in the library of every contemporary drummer.

RLP1 – Book w/2 CDs

Contemporary Drumset Techniques

by Rick Latham

The new edition of this book includes over four hours of audio to accompany the publication The CDs contain Latham performing all of the featured exercises as well as commentary and several short solo performances
RLP2 – Book w/4 CDs

Brushworks:
The New Language for Playing Brushes

Clayton Cameron

Legendary drummer Clayton Cameron reveals the secrets of good brushwork in this "must have" book that should be on every drummer's shelf. Noted as one of the wold's most innovative drummers, Cameron gives the reader an encyclopedic survey of brushstrokes in a step by step process with clear and precise notation designed especially for the brushes. Also included is a CD detailing the sounds and patterns in the book.
DRM105 – Book w/CD